DOES DEATH REALLY EXIST?

Swami Muktananda

About Swami Muktananda

Born in 1908 into a wealthy family in Mangalore, India, Swami Muktananda began his spiritual journey at the age of fifteen. A few years later he took the vows of a monk and was given the title Swami and the name Muktananda.

For twenty-five years he traveled around India on foot, spending time with many of the renowned saints and meditation masters of his day. He mastered the classical systems of Indian philosophy, as well as hatha yoga and many other branches of spiritual and worldly science. In 1947 he met Bhagawan Nityananda, one of the great modern saints of India and a master of the Siddha tradition. After nine years of intense study under Nityananda's guidance, Muktananda reached the goal of spiritual practice, the state of Self-realization.

When Nityananda died in 1961, he passed on the power of the Siddha lineage to Muktananda. Since that time Swami Muktananda has made several trips to the West and has introduced Siddha meditation to hundreds of thousands of people. He has a large international following, and his students have established several hundred meditation centers around the world.

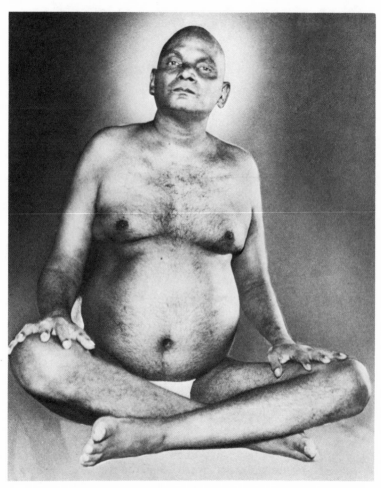

Swami Muktananda's Guru, Bhagawan Nityananda

Foreword

Death is the most universal and predictable fact of human existence. All of us, without exception, must confront the deaths of our relatives, friends, and acquaintances and ultimately our own biological demise. If the prospect of dying is the most certain thing in our lives, the timing of death is the most uncertain. We never know when and how it will come. One would expect that under these circumstances we would try to learn as much as we could about this phenomenon and prepare ourselves to face it at any time. Yet exactly the opposite seems to happen. The progress of Western civilization and the technological triumphs of mechanistic science have been accompanied by a profound and increasing denial of death. The average Westerner manages throughout his life to avoid coping with the issue of his mortality, either emotionally, philosophically, or spiritually. Therefore, when death approaches, he is caught completely by surprise.

This situation is exacerbated by the position to which contemporary science has relegated human consciousness. Materialistic science considers a human being to be a biological machine living in a material universe. Consciousness is seen simply as a product of physiological processes in the brain. It is therefore only logical that the destruction of the body and the brain should be considered the absolute end of the human being. This view is so basic to scientific understanding that anyone who asserts that consciousness exists independently of the body and beyond the point of physical death is assumed by Western scientists to be poorly educated, a wishful thinker, or even psychopathic.

Our treatment of people who are dying reflects this viewpoint. To the Western scientific mind, death is the ultimate indication of human failure. It is a painful reminder of the limits of our capacity to control nature and our own destiny. Contemporary medicine, with its overspecialized body mechanics and technological wizardry, regards death as something to be conquered, or at least delayed at any cost. As medical personnel struggle to prolong biological life, very little attention is paid to the patient's psychological, philosophical, and spiritual needs or to the quality of his remaining days. The old and the dying are removed to hospitals and nursing homes, where meaningful human contact is replaced by sophisticated gadgetry. Many of these people thus spend their time in the company of oxygen tents, infusion bottles and tubes, pacemakers, dialysis machines, and monitors of vital functions. It is not uncommon for a patient to have his life artificially maintained for years on end with the help of machinery as bizarre as any science fiction writer might imagine. Not only is the main emphasis of the medical profession on mechanical prolongation of organismic functions, but the patient's consciousness is frequently altered by drugs that not only dull pain, but also inhibit awareness of the process of dying.

A typical Westerner has to confront death entirely unprepared, isolated from meaningful social contacts, and imbued with the nihilistic spirit of materialistic philosophy. He or she faces the most profound of all crises — one that affects simultaneously the biological, emotional, philosophical, and spiritual dimensions of his or her being. Yet, until recently, the process of dying was systematically neglected by psychiatrists and psychologists. The mental health profession, which otherwise explored every other aspect of human life in minute and pedantic detail, offered no psychological help to the dying, showed no interest in the experiences accompanying dying, and considered the issue of death to be irrelevant for psychology, psychopathology, and psychotherapy.

This situation has changed dramatically in the last decade. As a result of the research of Elizabeth Kübler-Ross, Raymond Moody, and others, there is now vivid interest in death and dying among both professionals and the lay public. Psychiatric and psychological groups regularly hold symposia on thanatology, and many universities offer courses in this area. Many new articles and books on death and dying have appeared, and the issue has become a favorite of the mass media. But in spite of our acute awareness of the importance of death and dying, and in spite of all the work that has been done, we have not yet developed ways to relieve the suffering of those who are dying.

The fact is that thanatology is an area in which Westerners can learn much from ancient cultures and Eastern spiritual disciplines. In these traditions, an experiential knowledge of death is an integral part of the wisdom of life. The value of a profound confrontation with one's mortality has been explicitly acknowledged in such disparate frameworks as shamanism, rites of passage, ancient death – rebirth mysteries, and the spiritual practices of several great world religions. All these traditions share the belief that when we fully accept the mortality of that aspect of ourselves with which the ego identifies, we discover that our true identity is eternal and divine.

In this book, Swami Muktananda Paramahansa, one of the most respected spiritual teachers in the world, offers us the pure essence of an ancient tradition's wisdom about death. Swami Muktananda is a Siddha, a perfected master of one of the oldest and most honored spiritual lineages in the East. Through his own practice and through the grace and guidance of his Guru, Muktananda has reached a state commonly acknowledged as the pinnacle of human spiritual achievement, and it is this achievement that gives his teaching on death its power and authority.

Muktananda's contribution to the field of thanatology is profound and of fundamental relevance. He does not simply refine and amplify our existing knowledge, nor does he discuss ways to improve our current techniques of working with the dying. His is an entirely different approach, one that is as relevant for the living as for those facing imminent death. According to his teaching, suffering, whether in life or in death, is based on the ignorance of our own real nature and on a false sense of identity. Because we identify ourselves with our bodies and our social roles, we dread losing them; any extreme situation threatens their survival and consequently fills us with fear. But once we realize that our identity lies not in the ego or in the body, but in the subtle consciousness which operates through and beyond both, then our physical demise no longer represents to us the end of everything. In fact, when one gets to know one's real Self, not only does the fear of death disappear, but the suffering of life vanishes as well. To a person who knows the Self, both life and death become enjoyable games.

Drawing on the *Bhagavad Gita* and other classical texts of the Indian spiritual tradition, Swami Muktananda describes the life – death cycle in terms of the doctrine of *karma,* the ancient and immutable law of cause and effect, which decrees that one must experience the consequences of every action one performs. It is not that we are born and die only once; being born and dying are part of an endless cycle which comes to an end only when we discover the totally free consciousness that exists within us. We are prevented from experiencing this consciousness because of three impurities, which are the basic source of our false identification with the body and ego. These are *anavamala,* a painful sense of imperfection; *mayiyamala,* a tendency to experience oneself as a separate individual in a world of dualities; and *karmamala,* a sense of doership. Ultimately, the only means of freeing ourselves from these impurities, and from our consequent enslavement to the ego and the body, is spiritual practice. In short, spiritual endeavor, especially meditation, is the only effective way of liberating ourselves from the fear of death. Only if we have pursued such practice throughout our lives will we truly be able to die peacefully.

Here, Muktananda's teaching is fully in line with the doctrines of most Eastern traditions. What makes him unique as a teacher, however, is his ability to kindle the process of meditation within his students by directly awakening their inner purifying energy. That energy, called Kundalini in the ancient Indian texts, is recognized in virtually every spiritual tradition as the creative force of the universe and the life energy of the human organism. In a human being, this energy takes two forms. In its external form, it carries on all the functions of the organism. In its internal form, it gives rise to the spiritual process. However, in most people, the inner form of Kundalini is latent, lying dormant at the base of the spine. When awakened by a master like Muktananda, it begins to work on both a physical and subtle level, burning physical, emotional, and mental impurities and ultimately opening the individual to the experience of his or her innate nature. The final result of this process is the individual's transcendence of the ego and full identification with the Self, which is pure consciousness. This Self is all-pervading, indestructible, and eternal, and therefore it is not subject to birth and death. A human being who has become totally identified with and established in this consciousness finds nothing fearsome in the death of his physical body, because his overwhelming experience is of his own immortality.

Until recently, most Western scholars would have considered such a teaching to be entirely incompatible with science and rationality. However, recent developments in physics and in consciousness research have revealed far-reaching parallels between contemporary scientific discoveries and Eastern philosophical and spiritual systems. The Newtonian – Cartesian concepts of matter, space, time, and consciousness have undergone drastic changes. The universe is no longer seen as an essentially inert and unconscious mechanism, a gigantic supermachine assembled from separate material particles and objects, but as an infinitely complex, unified web of events and relations in which any boundaries are ephemeral and ultimately arbitrary. In this context, consciousness is not an insignificant epiphenomenon and product of material processes in the brain, but the primary aspect of existence. While the old mechanistic science was fundamentally irreconcilable with spiritual philosophy, modern science, approaching ancient wisdom from an independent perspective, demonstrates its validity more and more. Thus, there is no conflict between Muktananda's teaching and, for example, the contemporary holonomic theory of Bohm and Pribram, the "boot-strap" philosophy of nature of Geoffrey Chew, and the principles of Jungian psychology. But Muktananda's approach is far more radical and encompassing than any of these. It is not merely a theory or doctrine, but a teaching based on direct, repeatable experience, a teaching that, when practiced, can free us from our most deeply rooted fears and open us to undreamed-of freedom and joy. In this way, it is of incalculable value for all of us.

STANISLAUS GROF, M.D.

Dr. Grof is a psychiatrist who has done extensive work during the past twenty-five years on unusual states of consciousness. Former Chief of Psychiatric Research at the Maryland Psychiatric Research Center and Assistant Professor of Psychiatry at Johns Hopkins University, he is presently Scholar-in-Residence at Esalen Institute in Big Sur, California. He is the author of *Realms of the Human Unconscious* and co-author of *Beyond Death* and *The Human Encounter with Death.*

Swami Muktananda

If there is any truth in this world,
   if there is any greatness,
then it lies within a human being.
When God reveals Himself,
He does so within the human heart.
A human being is great;
he is sublime;
he is very high.
Of all the creatures
in the world,
a human being is the highest.

Why? Because he can earn money?
Even animals can work and earn money.
Because he eats and sleeps and procreates?
No, all other creatures
eat and sleep and procreate.

What is it, then,
which makes a human an ideal being?
Why is human birth so sublime?

1

If you ask a horse or a dog who he is,
he will not be able to tell you;
of all creatures, only a human being
has the capacity to know himself.
That is what is special
about human birth. If a person
does not use this birth to know himself,
to understand his own inner Consciousness,
then his life is wasted. A person's duty
is to find out who he is.

I did a great deal of *sadhana,*
or spiritual practice,
in graveyards. They are good for *sadhana*
because when you see all the dead bodies
you know that eventually
this is what will become of you.
A person sees his own future in a graveyard.
Every time I visit a graveyard,
I remember Kabir's poem:
"What is so remarkable about this body?
What is so remarkable about this mind?
What is so remarkable about your wealth
and everything else that you have?
As you are watching these things,
they fade into dust.
Look at your own life.
As you are watching it,
it just withers away."

This is my situation.
Once I was a young man. I did *sadhana.*
Now I am old, and I know
there is just a short time left
before I go home. As you are watching it,
your life merges into dust.

In India dead bodies are burned.
The hair goes up in flame like grass,
and the bones crackle like wood.
When this is the case,
what is so special about this body?
What is so wonderful about this mind?
Why does one want to cling to wealth?
In the end, none of these things matter
because they leave us when we die.
This is our fear in that last moment.
We are afraid
because we have to leave all of our supports behind
and go to meet God alone.
But what is so frightening about that?

People should understand
the reality of the world.
We fear death for no good reason.
Even if we fear death,
we are going to die anyway,
so why not accept it with courage?
If a person is brave in the face of death,

then when he is dying he feels
that he is just going to sleep.
He feels no torment.

I have watched many people die.
There was a time when I was very fond
of watching how people died.
I was present at the deaths
of three or four Siddhas,
fully realized beings, of five or six
pure-souled devotees of God,
and of five or six people
who had reached a state of even-mindedness.
I saw that death is not fearsome;
it is only that we worry about it.
Truly, death is nothing more
than a long sleep. The difference
is that in ordinary sleep
one knows that one is going to wake up,
whereas in the sleep of death
one does not wake up —
at least not in the same body.

The *Bhagavad Gita* says:
*jaatasya hi dhruvo mrutyur
dhruvam janma mrutasya cha;
tasmaad aparihaarye'rthe
na tvam shochitum arhasi.*[1]
"Certain is death for the born,

4

and certain is birth for the dead.
When one is born, death follows.
When one dies, rebirth follows."
The *Gita* also says:
vaasaamsi jeernaani yathaa vihaaya
navaani gruhnaati naro'paraani;
tathaa shareeraani vihaaya jeernaa
nyanyaani samyaati navaani dehee.[2]
"Just as a man casts off worn-out clothes
and gets new ones,
so the Self casts off worn-out bodies
and enters new ones."
When this is the case,
why does one worry? Why does one weep?
For a wise person, death is beautiful;
it is only when one lacks knowledge
that one fears it.

When one knows one's own Self,
death becomes an enjoyable game.
When Ramakrishna was dying,
one of his disciples asked him,
"The Divine Mother grants all your wishes.
Why don't you ask Her to cure your cancer?"
Ramakrishna replied,
"Why should I consider my cancer
a negative thing? Why shouldn't I consider it
the blessed gift of God?"
This is how a wise person dies.

There was a man
who used to come to our Ashram in India
every weekend from Bombay. At the end,
he developed a brain tumor.
That was his destiny, and destiny
does not leave anyone untouched.

I went to see this man
while he was in the hospital.
I asked him, "Are you in a lot of pain?"
He said, "No, by God's grace,
I have no pain." Then I asked him
if he wanted to have an operation
to remove the tumor, and he said, "No."
I asked him why, and he replied,
"I'm going to leave my body tomorrow."
Then I leaned over and whispered to him,
"I, too, feel that you are leaving,
and I'm very happy about it."
He said that he was also happy.

Very few people are happy about dying.
Most of us do not welcome death.
People know that they are going to die
eventually,
but they never want to die
right now, in this moment.
When most people die,
they become unconscious
and leave their bodies involuntarily.

The reason for this
is that the individual soul thinks,
"I am this body; I am a man;
I am a doctor; I experience this pleasure;
I experience that pain." He does not realize
that he is neither a man nor a woman,
neither the doer nor the experiencer of anything.
He does not understand that his true Self,
his innermost Consciousness,
is completely free from all bodies,
all pleasures, and all pain.
The *Bhagavad Gita* says:
nainam chindanti shastraani
nainam dahati paavakah;
na chainam kledayantyaapo
na shoshayati maarutah.[3]
"Weapons cut it not; fire burns it not;
water wets it not; wind dries it not."
Acchedyo'yam adaahyo'yam
akledyo'shoshya eva cha;
nityah sarvagatah sthaanur
achalo'yam sanaatanah.[4]
"This Self cannot be cut, burned,
wetted, nor dried up.
It is eternal, all-pervading,
stable, ancient, and immovable."
The Self is indestructible.
It can never die. A person who knows this
is not afraid to die; in fact,
he welcomes death. The people who wail,

"Oh, I am dying; what can I do now?"
are not really dying at all;
they are being dragged away by death.

I talked to the wife
of the Bombay devotee after he died,
and she described an interesting incident
that happened during his death.
She was sitting next to his bed
when the *prana*, the life force,
left his body, and she saw a blue dot —
a shimmering, shining, sparkling blue dot —
come out of one of his eyes
and go out of the hospital window.

This blue dot,
which we call the Blue Pearl,
dwells in the *sahasrara*,
the spiritual center
in the crown of the head.
It is the body of the Self.
All consciousness is contained in it.
All of the dynamism of the breathing process
comes from the Blue Pearl.
When that light enters the body,
the rhythm of breathing begins.
When it departs from the body,
consciousness departs from the bloodstream,
the nerves, and the lungs,

leaving everything limp and lifeless.
"Death" is simply the name we give
to the departure of the Blue Pearl from the body.

If a person dies
very beautifully, the soul can be seen
departing in the Blue Pearl.
Sometimes it leaves the body through the eyes,
sometimes the nose,
and sometimes the mouth.
Even if one does not see the soul depart,
one can usually tell
from which passage it left.
If it left through the eyes,
the eyes will be open wider.
If it left through the mouth,
the mouth will be open.
If a person has committed very bad actions,
his soul will leave through the anus,
and sometimes he will even excrete
out of fear. According to the scriptures,
this is a sign that he will go to hell.
If the soul leaves through a person's eyes,
then he has been very virtuous.

In our country,
at the time of death,
friends and relatives gather around
and recite the *Bhagavad Gita*

or chant the name of God.
If a dying person can be made
to turn to the divine name,
he can die peacefully,
because the name has so much power.
On the whole, however,
how a person dies is the fruit
of the way in which he has lived.
It is said that if you want to attain anything
in this life, attain a good death.
This is what great beings ask of God:
"O God, if You really want to give me something,
give me a good death, a sweet death."

What is there in worldly glory anyhow?
There have been so many important people,
but the world does not remember them.
There have been so many great kings,
but now they exist only in books.
Soon even the books will be gone.

I can tell you a story
about the death of a very wicked person,
the Moghul king Gajani Mahmoud.
He knew only two things:
how to steal and how to kidnap women.
In India the temples
are built with gold and precious gems.
Mahmoud took so much wealth

from India's temples
that he had to build enormous vaults
to hold all the diamonds, rubies, and pearls.

No matter who a person is,
death pursues him.
Whether he is a Mahmoud or a saint,
death does not spare him.
It does not come early
and it does not come late.
The moment of departure
is set at the time of birth,
and it does not change
by even a minute.
Death is the one thing in this world
that is always on time.

When his time came,
Mahmoud was in anguish.
As he lay on his deathbed,
all of his sins kept dancing before him.
He was squirming and suffering
from excruciating mental pain.
He cried out to the Muslim priest,
"Do something for me,"
but there was nothing anyone could do.
Only a person who performs good actions
can die peacefully, and Gajani Mahmoud
had committed many sins.

As he lay there writhing,
he told the people around him,
"There are three sins
staring me in the face.
Out of my greed for the throne,
I had my father slaughtered.
Out of lust, I murdered many women.
Then I tried to kill a great Guru;
in this I did not succeed.
The memory of these wicked deeds
will not let me die peacefully."

Before Mahmoud died,
he had his bed carried
into the treasure house,
where he could see the gems and gold
he had collected throughout his life.
Then he was taken to the harem
to look at his women.
When the women saw him,
they all turned their backs to him.
They would not show him their faces.
Finally Mahmoud called all of his ministers
and told them to warn people
not to live as he had lived.
He said, "When I die, open my hands
and let them hang outside the coffin,
and take my body through the villages
in a procession. Let the people see
that despite all the wealth

Gajani Mahmoud stole,
he left this world empty-handed."

Like Gajani Mahmoud,
we spend our lives seeking wealth.
We look for happiness
in our husbands or wives, our families,
our friends. We cling to our status,
our degrees, our positions,
and our possessions, and we feel
that they give meaning to our lives.
Yet when we leave this world,
we take none of these things with us.
Kabir wrote:
"O friend, you build such a big mansion,
yet in the end you will go and sleep in the jungle."
In the *Bhagavad Gita,*
the Lord describes two kinds of wealth:
worldly wealth and divine wealth.
Worldly wealth exists only here
in this world. It has no value
after we leave our bodies.
Divine wealth takes us to God.
Divine wealth is our love,
our compassion for others,
our devotion to God. It enables us
to attain happiness and peace in this world,
and it goes with us when we leave.
Divine wealth buys God.
Worldly wealth buys only death.

When a person
is about to die, all his actions —
good or bad, virtuous or sinful —
appear as images before him.
There are two paths after death.
One is filled with light and joy,
and the other with darkness and fear.
Very naturally, we take one or the other.
According to our actions,
God decides what we will experience after death.

When a great person
comes to visit, we greet him with pomp:
we send a limousine to meet him and give him flowers.
In the same way, when a good soul is dying,
the deities come to escort him,
and his path is filled
with light and beauty and joy.
The soul goes to the ancestral plane,
and the actions he has committed during his life
are evaluated there.
On the other hand,
when a person has committed a murder
in this world, a policeman handcuffs him
and takes him to jail. In the same way,
when a person who is evil
and has committed many sins must die,
low beings come to take him through a channel
filled with darkness and fear,
and his journey is one of horror.

In India there is a custom:
when a person's parents die,
he immediately gives things away in charity.
He holds a large feast,
and at that time gives money to the poor
and distributes shoes, clothing, cattle,
or whatever else he has. He does all this
and performs rituals and ceremonies
so that his parents
can attain the world of ancestors.

If a person
has been extremely virtuous on earth,
then when he dies he attains heaven.
Heaven is the world of sense pleasures;
even in America there are not
such sense pleasures as there are in heaven.
But just as the pleasures of this life pass,
so do the pleasures of heaven.
As long as one has a fund of merits,
one can enjoy them,
but the moment one's merits are spent,
one must leave heaven and be reborn.
In the same way,
a person who has committed many sins
attains a world in which he suffers very much.
However, once he has undergone
the consequences of his bad actions,
he too is thrown back to this world.
Whether one goes to heaven or to hell,
one is reborn.

15

In this world,
whether or not a person likes it
he has to accept the decision of a judge.
In the same way, when a person dies,
whether or not he likes it
he has to abide by the judgment of God.
Some people think that there is no maker,
no master, of this world,
that everything happens of its own accord.
But there is a maker of all this.
There is a master,
and his law is completely just.
We reap the consequences of our own actions.
This is God's law: the law of *karma.*
Karma literally means "action."
According to the law of *karma,*
every action produces a reaction.
This means that all our actions —
mental and verbal, as well as physical —
bear fruit. In the *Bhagavad Gita*
it is said, *gahanaa karmano gatih,*[5]
"The ways of *karma* are unfathomable,"
and this is true. But the hard fact is
that one receives the fruits of one's actions
from God, and the fruits always correspond
to the actions.
This body is like a field.
Whatever we sow is what will sprout
and what we will harvest. If we sow
lemon seeds in a field,

we will not harvest mangos.
In the same way, if we sow
bad actions in the field of the body,
we will not harvest good fruits.
Therefore, we must be conscious
when we are performing actions.
Whenever we hurt someone,
we should be aware
that we are really hurting ourselves.
We should perform only good actions.

We take birth
according to our actions.
The circumstances of our present birth
were determined by our actions
in past lives. There are people
who do not believe in rebirth,
but whether or not they believe in it,
they still have to suffer
the consequences of their actions.
The most powerful proof of reincarnation
is the knowledge that comes to us in meditation.
As we meditate more and more,
we are able to see very clearly —
just as clearly as we see objects
in our everyday existence —
who we were in past lives,
who our parents were, and where we lived.
There is a fort in Maharashtra State in India
which I used to visit when I was young.

I felt a strange fascination for it;
I was drawn back to it again and again,
and each time I went there I would weep.
I could not understand the depth
of my attachment to that fort.
Then in meditation I saw that in a past life
I had lived there as a king.
I have seen several of my past lives in meditation.
For me, there is no greater
proof of reincarnation than that.

The inequalities
we can see in different people
from the very moment of birth
are further proof of reincarnation.
Six children born of the same parents
all grow individually with different constitutions,
different temperaments, different talents,
and different ways. This is an indication
that they must each have been born
with different *karmas*.

The world is without beginning,
and so is our store of *karma*.
A person may appear
to be twenty or thirty or forty years old,
but in fact he is ageless.
Even though we were born
in our present forms only a few years ago,

the essential spirit within has existed
from time without beginning. Thus,
the accumulated store of our past *karma*
is inconceivably vast. It is this past *karma*
which brings us happiness and sorrow,
pleasure and pain, and which binds us to life.
We are born, and we die.
We are reborn, and we die again.
We transmigrate through different life forms,
high and low. As we exhaust
our *karma* of the past, we create
new *karma* for the future.

How can a person free himself
from this wheel of death and rebirth?
He can do so only by going within
and, through meditation, discovering
his own inner Self. As we meditate,
we become established
in the seat of the inner Self,
and then we are liberated from death.
In meditation, we discard our individual ego
and merge with the Self.
The ego is a veil which hides the Self
and keeps us bound to the body.
The ego is nothing but our sense
of limited individuality, our identification
with the body and the mind, with our sex,
our family, our country, our position.

Although the Self is completely stainless,
when it is enveloped in the three impurities
the ego is born, and we become bound.

In Kashmir Shaivism,
the three impurities are described
in great detail. A grain of rice
is covered by three layers —
an outer husk and two inner coverings.
When one removes all three layers,
one is left with a pure grain of rice.
One can eat this pure rice,
but if one sows it, it will not sprout.
It cannot grow because it does not have
those three coverings.
Similarly, an individual being
is covered by three impurities
called the three *malas:*
anavamala, mayiyamala, and *karmamala.*
Anavamala is the awareness of imperfection,
mayiyamala is the awareness of duality,
and *karmamala* is the awareness of doership.
These *malas* come into being
through the contraction of our great powers
of will, knowledge, and action —
iccha, jnana, and *kriya.*
When these powers are fully expanded,
we are able to will anything,
we are omniscient,
and we can carry out any action.

When they contract, we feel limited,
we know only illusion,
and we are able to perform only a few actions.
We feel imperfect. We feel agitated.
We feel attachment and aversion and anger
within ourselves. Because of the three *malas,*
an individual soul is born again and again.
When the *malas* are removed
through spiritual practices
and the grace of a pure being,
the individual soul goes beyond birth and death
and is never again reborn.

The purpose of spiritual life
is to become free of these impurities,
and to do that we must perform
only good actions. If we perform bad actions —
if we hurt ourselves or other people —
then over and over again
we are enveloped by these *malas.*
As long as we are covered by them,
we are mere human beings.
But once we become free of them,
we are nothing but Supreme Consciousness.

Within every human being
is a great and divine energy called Kundalini.
This energy has created
the entire universe in total freedom.

It pervades the universe,
and it also pervades the human body
and makes it function.
This energy has two aspects.
Its outer aspect is awake
and functioning perfectly;
it is this which enables us to carry on
all our mundane activities. However,
the inner, spiritual aspect of this energy
is dormant. When it is awakened
through the grace of the Guru,
a spontaneous process begins within.
Then the awakened energy
moves through our system, burning
all the impurities in the body.
Through the meditation which takes place
after Kundalini awakening,
one easily comes to see the Self within the heart.
The fire of that knowledge of the Self
destroys the three *malas*,
and one expands more and more.
Once one has completely evolved,
one knows, "I am God."
Instead of having the awareness
that one is the body,
one very naturally becomes aware,
"I am the Self." When one realizes
that God dwells within
as one's own inner Self,
the fire of that knowledge
burns all one's accumulated *karma*.

If we think about it,
we will realize that even in daily life
we have the experience
of going beyond the body.
At night we go to sleep,
and the experiences of the waking state
do not exist in the dream state.
In dreams we experience so many strange worlds,
but when we awaken,
these worlds no longer exist.
In the deep sleep state
we go beyond these first two states
and become immersed in oblivion.
Our own experience shows us
that there is something beyond this physical body.
When we talk about the body,
what do we say? Do we say,
"This is my body," or do we say,
"I am this body"? To say, "I am this body,"
would be like saying, "I am this towel,"
or "I am this hat." When we say,
"This is my body," we demonstrate
that we are different from the body.
The sages of the Upanishads asked the question,
"Who is it that perceives
all the different events of the waking state?
Who is it that remains awake
when we are sleeping and,
when we wake up, reports to us on our dreams?"
That being, that witness who watches everything

while remaining separate from it,
is the Self. In the Upanishads it is said
that the knower of our waking and dream states,
the witness of our thoughts and feelings,
is nothing but pure Consciousness,
the Absolute, Brahman.
This is what we discover in meditation.

As we meditate, we move beyond
the waking, dream, and deep sleep states
to the transcendental state.
The scriptures tell us
that we do not have one body, but four.
The first is the gross physical body,
in which we experience the waking state.
When we move beyond the physical body,
we enter the subtle body, in which we dream.
Beyond the subtle body is the causal body,
which is the body of the deep sleep state.
Beyond all these bodies lies the fourth body,
the body of the transcendental state.
The fourth body is the Blue Pearl,
the subtlest covering of the individual soul,
and when we see this tiny blue light in meditation,
we should understand that we are seeing
the form of the inner Self.
To experience this is the goal of human life.
The Blue Pearl is also called the supracausal body.
It is tiny, but it contains
all the different planes of existence.

In meditation I traveled to the world of death
and the world of ancestors,
where I saw many people I knew.
I also visited heaven and hell,
which are real places apart from the heaven and hell
we make for ourselves in this world.
Heaven is a city of extraordinary beauty
where trees bear blossoms of many colors
and the wind is laden with divine fragrances.
Hell is a land of utter filth and misery,
filled with excreta.

U ltimately,
as one meditates and meditates,
one becomes established
in the transcendental state.
But before that happens, one experiences
one's own death while still alive.
The great being Tukaram Maharaj said,
"I have seen my own death with my own eyes,"
and he was speaking the truth.
In meditation a yogi can see the soul
leaving the body
and moving farther and farther away.
One day in meditation I saw a light
as brilliant as the light of millions of suns.
As I gazed at it, I felt it draw me
toward itself.
I was overcome with fear.

My *prana* stopped moving,
and I cried out and fell unconscious.
I lay in this state for some time,
and then I got up
filled with peace and love. I realized
that I had had the experience of death;
I understood that death
is nothing more than the experience I had had
after seeing that light.
From that moment,
there was no more fear of death for me.
Once one has had that experience,
one is never again afraid of death.
Therefore, when the moment comes
to die in meditation, one should die completely.
Then one will come back to life in such a way
that one will never die again.
Individual existence is a thin veil,
and supreme bliss lies just beyond it.
Tear off that veil. Hunt death,
and then see what happens.
You will see that death itself has died.
Once you have experienced
the death of your individuality,
you will become immortal.

The truth is that it is our own ego
which is death for us.
When we have gone beyond the ego,

death no longer exists.
The great being Ram Tirth told a story
which illustrates this very beautifully.
Once there was a yogi
who had done a great deal of *sadhana*
and had attained the ability to multiply himself
into forty identical forms.
He became very famous for this *siddhi*.
Many people would come to see him,
and he was considered a great being.
Eventually the time came when he had to die.
Because of his yogic powers,
he understood that death was approaching.
As soon as he knew that the messenger of death
was on his way, he multiplied himself
into forty identical forms.
When the messenger saw the forty yogis,
he became completely confused.
He could not tell which of the forms
was the one he had come for,
so he returned to the kingdom of death.
He told Yama, the god of death, what had happened.
Yama called another messenger,
who was more intelligent than the first one.
He whispered some instructions in his ear
and sent him off to the yogi's place.

Once again the yogi knew
that death's messenger was coming for him,

and once again
he multiplied himself into forty forms.
When the messenger entered the room
and saw the forty yogis standing in a line,
he began to shake his head in admiration.
He walked around and around,
inspecting them from every angle.
"Wow, wow," he said.
"How perfect! How magnificent!
What a miraculous piece of work."
The yogi was already full of pride,
but when he heard these words of praise
he became completely inflated.
Then the messenger stopped in front of the line.
He frowned slightly and said,
"There is just one tiny flaw."
"What flaw?" the yogi cried.
And the messenger of death grabbed him.

In the same way,
our ego brings us again and again to our death.
In order to conquer death,
we have to transcend the ego,
to overcome our limited individuality.
We have to realize our identity
with the Universal Consciousness.
We have to merge with that Consciousness,
just as a river merges with the ocean.
When a being has attained this state of oneness,

he has gone beyond death.
The *Gita* says:
*gunaan etaan ateetya treen
dehee dehasamudbhavaan;
janma mrutyu jaraa duhkhair
vimukto'amrutam ashnute.*[6]
"The embodied one,
having gone beyond the three *gunas*
out of which the body is evolved,
is freed from birth, death, decay, and pain
and attains immortality."

When an individual person dies,
the soul leaves the body
and adopts the next form
according to his *karma.*
In the case of the great beings
who have become one with the highest Reality,
the *prana* does not leave the body
as it does with ordinary people.
In the Upanishads it is said
that at the time of a saint's final *samadhi,*[7]
the *prana* merges in the *sahasrara*
and does not leave the body. For such a one,
the cycle of birth and death is ended.
The poems of saints say
that one can know a true yogi
by the way he dies.

Zipruanna was a great, omniscient being
whom I used to visit frequently.
He was always naked,
and he would sleep on heaps of garbage
because for him everything
was a velvet bed.
One day when I was leaving him,
he walked me all the way
to the edge of the village.
He mentioned the name of a place
where I should stay, and then he stood
and waved good-bye to me
for as long as I could see him.

Eight days later he left his body.
When I heard about his death,
I understood why he had given me
such a send-off.
He had known he would die.
If one prays to the inner divinity
very intensely, one comes to know
when one will die. Usually a yogi
finds out about his death
three months before it occurs.
In India there have been many yogis
who have prepared their own tombs.
They have sat in the place they have chosen,
closed their eyes,
and left their bodies.

After hearing of Zipruanna's death,
I went to visit the woman
in whose house he had died.
She was a schoolteacher named Jyoshi,
and she had great love for her Zipru.
That day he had come to her house and told her,
"I want to eat some rice and milk."
She was very pleased,
because he never requested anything of anyone.
She made him a particular sweet
of rice boiled in milk,
and he ate a little of it,
leaving the rest for her.
Then he said,
"First massage my body with oil,
and then heat some water.
I want to take a bath."
As far as anyone knew,
he had never taken a bath
in his entire life.
Jyoshi heated some water for him,
and after he had bathed he said,
"Now your Zipru is leaving.
You can cry as much as you like."
With that, he died.
This is how a Siddha leaves his body.

It was like this
when my own Guru, Bhagawan Nityananda, left.
One August night in 1961

he called me to him
and put his hand on my head.
Then he whispered something to me.
He put his hand in my mouth
and gave me the final *diksha,*
the initiation of the Siddhas.
I knew immediately
that he was going to leave his body soon.
I became as still as a tree.
We sat there for a long time:
I motionless,
and he with his hand on my head.
I can still feel the place where it rested.
Then at about eleven o'clock he said, "Go."
I sat outside for a while,
just getting used to the idea
that he was going to leave his body.
Then I spent the rest of the night
calling people:
"Babaji's not feeling well.
If you want to see him, come soon."

The next morning, many people were there.
He was lying flat on his cot,
talking a bit to everyone
as I massaged his feet.
As I was massaging them,
his legs stretched out.
During his last years,

he had suffered from arthritis
because throughout his life
he had been used to lying down anywhere,
on stones or on the bare ground.
Before that moment, he had not been able
to stretch out his legs,
but at the time of his death,
they stretched out straight.
Our scriptures say
that when our bad *karma* is exhausted,
it leaves us, and I saw
an example of this at that moment.

At about nine o'clock,
Baba's eyes opened wide and he looked
at everyone in the room individually.
His body did not move at all,
but we could see the *prana* moving upward.
First the life left his feet;
then his legs became limp.
I took his hand and then that too
became cold. Finally his eyes rolled up
into his head. The *sushumna* nerve
vibrated between his eyebrows. At the very end,
he made the sound *Om.*
That was it. My Guru had died.
In his death I saw what the scriptures describe;
his *prana* did not leave his body.
Such beings are very rare.

The *Bhagavad Gita* describes two paths
by which a yogi can leave his body.
By one of these paths,
he merges with the Absolute;
by the other, he returns
through future births.
Agnirjyotirahah shuklah
shanmaasaa uttaraayanam;
tatra prayaataa gacchanti
brahma brahmavido janaah. [8]
"Fire, light, day, the bright [half of the month],
the six months of the northern path [of the sun];
going forth at these times,
those who know the Absolute
go to the Absolute."

In his commentary on this verse,
Jnaneshwar Maharaj says:
"So, O great warrior, listen to Me.
At the crisis of death,
the five elements leave the body last.
If at the moment of dying
reason is not overcome by confusion,
memory does not become blind,
and the mind does not become deadened,
then the organs of perception retain their vigor,
and the union with the Eternal
which one has experienced
becomes a protective sheath.

"In this way,
the senses remain conscious.
This condition lasts till death supervenes.
But this is possible
only so long as the heat of the body
is maintained. If our lamp has been extinguished
by wind or water,
is the sight of our eyes of any use to us?
Similarly, at the time of death,
the body becomes full of mucus
because of the action of the bodily wind,
and the spark of the inner fire is put out.
When the life energy is lost, what can reason do?
Consciousness, therefore, cannot remain active
in the body without heat.
O beloved, when the fire in the body ceases,
then the body is no longer a body,
but merely a lump of damp clay.
The life span struggles in vain to find its end
in the darkness.
At this time, one has to preserve all memories
of the past and, leaving the body,
attain union with Brahman.
The perception of consciousness is drowned
in the phlegm of the body,
and all awareness of past and future ceases.
Therefore, the benefit accruing
from the previous practice of yoga is lost
even before death occurs,
as though the lamp held in the hand were extinguished

before one had found what was lost.
Know then that the gastric fire
is the basis of consciousness.
This fire is the source of all strength
at the moment of death.

"Within, there should be the light of the gastric fire;
without, the time should be
the bright half of the month,
during daytime,
and during one of the six months
of the northern path of the sun.
He who gives up his body
under the conjunction of such auspicious conditions
becomes one with the Eternal,
for he is a knower of Brahman.
Listen now, O wielder of the bow,
such is the power of this conjunction,
and hence this is the straight path
by which it is possible to reach Me.
Here the gastric fire is the first step,
the light of the fire the second,
the daytime the third,
and the bright half of the month the fourth.
The requirement
of one of the six months of the northern path
is the highest step of this ascent
by which the yogi arrives at the place of perfection
in union with Brahman.
This is known to be the best time,

and it is called the bright path.
Now listen
and I will describe to you
the inauspicious time."[9]

Dhoomo raatristathaa krishnah
shanmaasaa dakshinaayam;
tatra chaandramasam jyotir
yogee praapya nivartate. [10]
"Smoke, night,
so also the dark [half of the month],
the six months of the southern path [of the sun];
going forth at such a time,
the yogi obtains the lunar light
and returns."

"At the moment of dying
the heart is compressed in darkness,
owing to the pressure of air and phlegm.
The sense organs are blocked,
memory is lost in confusion,
the mind becomes bewildered,
and the life force is constricted.
The fire of the gastric juices
becomes extinguished
and smoke pervades everywhere.
For this reason, consciousness is confined within the body,
just as when heavy clouds hide the moon
there is neither brilliance nor darkness
but only a dim light.

Thus, a person neither dies,
nor remains conscious. He becomes motionless;
his earthly life awaits the moment of death.

"When a mist has spread over
the sense organs, the mind, and the intellect,
all the gains of life are lost.
When a person loses
whatever he has possessed,
what value is there in gaining anything more?
Such is this person's state at the moment of death.
This is the condition in the body.
Externally, the time is night,
in the dark half of the month,
during one of the six months of the southern path.
If all these, which bring about rebirth
in the cycle of birth and death,
come together at a man's dying moment,
how can he attain union with Brahman?
Dying at such a juncture,
a yogi reaches the moon-world,
and then he descends again into earthly existence.
Know that I have spoken here
of the inauspicious time, O son of Pandu;[11]
this is the dark path leading to the recurrence of birth.
The other, called the path of light,
is the busy high road, straight and easy,
leading to Self-realization."[12]

Shuklakrishne gatee hyete
jagatah shashvate mate;
ekayaa yaatyanaavruttim
anyayaavartate punah.[13]
"Light and darkness,
these paths are thought to be
the world's everlasting paths.
By the one, one goes not to return;
by the other, one returns again."

"O Arjuna, these are the two everlasting paths,
one straight and the other crooked.
I have purposely pointed them out to you
so that for your welfare
you can see the right path and the wrong,
recognize the true and the false,
and know what is good and what is harmful.
Is a person likely to plunge into deep water
when he sees a good boat near him?
Will a person go by a side path
when he knows the right road?
Will a person who can distinguish between
nectar and poison be able to give up the nectar?
Likewise, one who sees a straight road
will not take a side path.
So one should discriminate clearly between good and evil,
and then one will avoid the inauspicious moment."[14]

One's condition at the time of death
is the result of one's actions.
Therefore, one must meditate.
Meditation on the Self is the greatest
of all good actions.
Just as one goes to sleep at night,
wakes up in the morning,
bathes, eats breakfast, goes to work,
and takes care of one's possessions,
so one should meditate.
The great being Bartruhari said,
"As long as the body is healthy,
as long as old age is far away,
as long as your senses are strong,
you should remember the Lord."
Waiting until one is dying to save oneself
is like trying to dig a well
when one's house is on fire.
If one wants to die peacefully,
one must begin helping oneself
long before one's time to die has come.

One should understand the value of time
and, with this understanding,
meditate and repeat God's name.
A person can attain everything in this world,
but once time has passed
he cannot get it back.
Everyone must die.
We must remain aware of this

40

because we have to prepare ourselves well
for the final journey.
We have made that journey
through many lifetimes.
A wise person contemplates this
and lives his life with the awareness
that death will come one day.
A great being said, "There are two things
you must remember all the time.
One is God, and the other
is your own death." In the *Gita*, when describing
the characteristics of a wise person,
the Lord says that he is one who has
janma mrutyu jaraa vyaadhi
duhkha doshaanudarshanam, [15]
"perception of the evils of birth, death,
old age, sickness, and pain."

The great being Shankaracharya sang:
punarapi jananam punarapi maranam,
punarapi jananee jathare shayanam. [16]
"One is born and one dies.
One is reborn and one dies again.
One comes into a mother's womb
again and again."
If we want final deliverance
from this treadmill,
we must meditate.
We must remember God.
Always be vigilant.

41

Wake up before death comes and surprises you.
In order to die peacefully,
you must meditate and remember the Lord.
This is what the Lord says in the *Gita:*
antakaale cha maameva
smaran muktvaa kalevaram;
yah prayaati sa madbhaavam
yaati naastyatra samshayah. [17]
"Whoever at the time of death
goes forth from the body remembering Me alone,
attains My being."

But how will we be able to remember Him
in the face of the tremendous fear
that grips us at the last moment of our life?
We will be able to do it only
if we have developed the habit of remembering Him
long before that time.
Yam yam vaapi smaran bhaavam
tyajatyante kalevaram;
tam tam evaiti kaunteya
sadaa tabdhaavabhaavitah. [18]
"Whatever being a person thinks of
at the last moment
when he leaves his body,
that alone does he attain."
Therefore,
whatever is in one's mind
at that moment of death
is extremely significant.

For this reason
we hold regular recitation of sacred texts
at our Ashrams.
If one memorizes
good words, they keep reverberating inside.
If one studies the *Bhagavad Gita,*
the Bible, and the Upanishads,
they keep coming to one's mind.
One who remembers God constantly in this way
will attain the state of God
at the time of death.
One who meditates and prays every day
has no fear of death.

I n the morning the sun rises,
and in the evening the sun sets.
In the morning we get up,
eat, go to work, talk to friends.
In the evening we go back home and sleep.
We do not realize how time deceives us.
The years go by,
and we celebrate one birthday after another.
We do not understand
that we are losing those years;
we only remember the celebrations.
Kabir Sahib wrote:
"You spent your time without chanting God's name.
You spent your childhood days in play.
When the heat of youth entered you,

you spent your time seeking honor and wealth
and indulging your senses.
You forgot the reason you came into this world.
You nourished your desires,
which increased and increased
and consumed your life.
You spent your time without chanting God's name."

We forget to contemplate,
"Who am I? Why was I born?
What is the goal of my life?
What am I supposed to accomplish here?"
We forget the reason we are here,
and so we eat and drink and make merry.
We indulge in sense pleasures,
and one day we leave this body.
Kabir wrote:
"O friend, listen to me:
through chanting God's name,
great beings go across the ocean of this world."
We can all go across in this way.
One day the body will drop away.
In this world, everything that comes
also goes.
But the Self does not die.
The inner Self is ageless and unchanging.
Death cannot reach it.
Therefore, live with this awareness:
"The Supreme Truth lies within me;

the flame of Supreme Truth is shimmering
and shining inside me."
That light is the Self.

May your awareness turn inward.
May you live with the knowledge,
"I am the Supreme Truth;
pure Consciousness lies within me."
Through the fire of this knowledge,
may death die for you.
I wish this for you all.

Your own,

स्वामी मुक्तानंद.

Swami Muktananda

NOTES

[1]*Bhagavad Gita,* II, 27.

[2]Ibid., 22.

[3]Ibid., 23.

[4]Ibid., 24.

[5]Ibid., IV, 17.

[6]Ibid., XIV, 20.

[7]The passing of a yogi is referred to as his *maha samadhi* or final *samadhi.*

[8]*Bhagavad Gita,* VIII, 24.

[9]Jnaneshwar, *Jnaneshwari,* VIII, 206 – 223.

[10]*Bhagavad Gita,* VIII, 25.

[11]It should be noted that for a Siddha like Nityananda there is no question of auspicious or inauspicious moments. A Siddha merges with the Absolute no matter when he dies.

[12]Jnaneshwar, *Jnaneshwari,* VIII, 224 – 235.

[13]*Bhagavad Gita,* VIII, 26.

[14]Jnaneshwar, *Jnaneshwari,* VIII, 236 – 240.

[15]*Bhagavad Gita,* XIII, 8.

[16]Shankaracharya, *Carpatapanjarika Stotram.*

[17]*Bhagavad Gita,* VIII, 5.

[18]Ibid., 6.

Glossary

Ashram: An institution or community where spiritual discipline is practiced; the abode of a saint or holy man.

Bhagavad Gita: A portion of the *Mahabharata* and one of the great works of spiritual literature, in which Lord Krishna explains the path of liberation to Arjuna on the battlefield during the war described in the epic poem.

Bhartruhari: A king who left his throne to become a yogi. He is especially noted for his poems on the theme of renunciation, which are collected in the *Vairagya Shataka.*

Gunas: Three basic qualities of nature, which combine to produce everything in the universe. They are *sattva,* purity; *rajas,* activity; and *tamas,* inertia.

Jnaneshwar Maharaj (1275 – 1296): Foremost among the saints of Maharashtra and a child yogi of extraordinary powers. He was born into a family of saints, and his older brother Nivrittinath was his Guru. His verse commentary on the *Bhagavad Gita* — *Jnaneshwari* —

written in the Marathi language, is acknowledged as one of the most important spiritual works. He took live *samadhi* at the age of 21 in Alandi, where his *samadhi* shrine continues to attract thousands of seekers.

Kabir (1440–1518): A great poet-saint who lived his life as a weaver in Benares. His followers were both Hindus and Muslims, and his influence was a strong force in overcoming religious factionalism.

Kashmir Shaivism: Nondual philosophy that recognizes the entire universe as a manifestation of Chiti, or divine conscious energy. Kashmir Shaivism explains how the formless, unmanifest Supreme Principle manifests as the universe. The authoritative scripture is the *Shiva Sutras.*

Krishna (lit. the dark one; the one who attracts irresistibly): The eighth incarnation of Vishnu, whose life story is described in the *Shrimad Bhagavatam* and the *Mahabharata* and whose spiritual teachings are contained in the *Bhagavad Gita.*

Kundalini (lit. coiled one): The primordial Shakti, or cosmic energy, that lies coiled in the *muladhara chakra* of every individual. When awakened, Kundalini begins to move upward within the *sushumna,* the subtle central channel, piercing the *chakras* and initiating various yogic processes which bring about total purification and rejuvenation of the entire being. When Kundalini enters the *sahasrara,* the spiritual center in the crown of the head, the individual self merges in the universal Self and attains the state of Self-realization.

Prana: Vital force; also the inhalation in the breathing process. Within the body, there are five major *pranas* —*prana, apana, vyana, udana,* and *samana.*

Ramakrishna (1836 – 1886): Great saint of modern India; the Guru of Vivekananda.

Sadhana: The practice of spiritual discipline.

Sahasrara: Thousand-petaled spiritual center at the crown of the head where one experiences the highest states of consciousness.

Samadhi: The superconscious state of oneness with the Absolute.

Shankaracharya (788 – 820): One of the greatest of India's philosophers and sages, who expounded the philosophy of absolute nondualism (Advaita Vedanta). In addition to his writing and teaching, he established *maths* (ashrams) in the four corners of India.

Siddha: A perfected yogi; one who has attained the highest state and become one with the Absolute.

Siddhi: Supernatural power.

Sushumna: The central nerve, or *nadi*, situated within the spinal column. The awakened Kundalini makes its journey within the *sushumna.*

Tukaram Maharaj (1608 – 1650): Great poet-saint of Maharashtra; author of thousands of *abhangas* (devotional songs).

Upanishads: The teachings of the ancient sages which form the knowledge or end portion of the Vedas. The central doctrine is that the Self of a human being is the same as Brahman, the Absolute. The goal of life is realization of Brahman.

OTHER PUBLICATIONS

By Swami Muktananda

The Perfect Relationship   The Guru/disciple relationship
Secret of the Siddhas   Swami Muktananda on Siddha Yoga and Kashmir Shaivism
Mystery of the Mind   How to deal with the mind
Reflections of the Self   Poems of spiritual life
Play of Consciousness   Muktananda's spiritual autobiography
Satsang with Baba   (Five Volumes) Questions and answers
Muktananda-Selected Essays   Edited by Paul Zweig
Meditate   Muktananda's basic teaching on meditation
In the Company of a Siddha   Muktananda talks with pioneers in science, con-
  sciousness and spirituality
Light on the Path   Essential aspects of the Siddha path
Siddha Meditation*   Commentaries on the Shiva Sutras and other ancient texts
Mukteshwari I & II   Poetic aphorisms
I Am That   The science of Hamsa mantra
Kundalini: The Secret of Life   Muktananda's teachings on our innate
  spiritual energy
**Small books of aphorisms: I Welcome You All With Love, God Is With You, A
  Book for the Mind, I Love You*, and To Know the Knower.**

About Swami Muktananda

A Search for the Self   by Swami Prajnananda. Swami Muktananda's biography
Muktananda Siddha Guru*   by Shankar (Swami Shankarananda). Introduction to
  Muktananda and his teachings

Other Books

Introduction to Kashmir Shaivism   The philosophy most closely reflecting Muk-
  tananda's teaching
Understanding Siddha Yoga, Volumes I & II   Textbooks on Siddha Yoga
Nectar of Chanting   Sacred chants sung regularly in Muktananda's Ashrams.
  Sanskrit translation with transliteration
Lalleshwari   Poems of a great woman saint
Hatha Yoga for Meditators   A detailed guide to Hatha Yoga as taught in Swami
  Muktananda's Ashrams
Shree Guru Gita   Word-by-word translation with transliteration and original Sanskrit

Publications

Gurudev Siddha Peeth Newsletter   Monthly from Muktananda's Ashram in India
Shree Gurudev Vani   Annual Journal by devotees
Siddha Path   Monthly magazine of SYDA Foundation

* Also available in Braille   Complete with photographs

If you want more information about these books, write to SYDA Bookstore,
P.O. Box 605, South Fallsburg, N.Y. 12779.

MAJOR CENTERS AND ASHRAMS

There are over 300 Siddha Yoga Meditation Centers and residential Ashrams around the world. They all hold regular programs which are free and open to the public. Many of them also conduct Siddha Yoga Meditation Intensives and Introductory Programs. Contact any of the following major Centers for the location of the Center nearest you.

UNITED STATES

SYDA Foundation New York
P.O. Box 600
South Fallsburg, New York 12799
Phone: (914)434-2000/(212)247-5997

SYDA Foundation Ann Arbor
1520 Hill
Ann Arbor, Michigan 48104
Phone: (313)994-5625/994-3072

SYDA Foundation Boston
Fernwood Road—Manor House
Chestnut Hill, Massachusetts 02167
Phone: (617)734-0137

**Siddha Yoga Meditation
Ashram Chicago**
2100 W. Bradley Place
Chicago, Illinois 60618
Phone: (312)327-0536

Siddha Yoga Dham Gainesville
1000 SW 9th Street
Gainesville, Florida 32601
Phone: (904)375-7629

Siddha Yoga Dham Hawaii
P.O. Box 10191
Honolulu, Hawaii 96816
3807 Diamond Head Circle
Honolulu, Hawaii 96815
Phone: (808)732-1558

**Muktananda Meditation Center
Siddha Yoga Dham Houston**
3815 Garrott
Houston, Texas 77006
Phone: (713)529-0006

**Siddha Yoga Meditation Center
Costa Mesa**
431 East 20th Street
Costa Mesa, CA 92627
Phone: (714)631-4446

SYDA Foundation Manhattan
324 West 86th Street
New York, New York 10024
Phone: (212)873-8030

Siddha Yoga Dham Miami
256 S.W. 12th Street
Miami, Florida 33130
Phone: (305)858-5369

SYDA Foundation Oakland
P.O. Box 11071
Oakland, California 94611
1107 Stanford Avenue
Oakland, California 94608
Phone: (415)655-8677

Siddha Yoga Dham Philadelphia
6429 Wayne Avenue
Philadelphia, Pennsylvania 19119
Phone: (215)849-0888

Siddha Yoga Dham Seattle
1409 N.E. 66th
Seattle, Washington 98115
Phone: (206)523-2583

**Siddha Yoga Dham
Washington, D.C.**
5015 16th St. N.W.
Washington, D.C. 20011
Phone: (202)882-4377

AUSTRALIA

Siddha Yoga Dham Melbourne
202 Gore Street
Fitzroy, Melbourne VIC 3065
Australia
Phone: (03)419-6299

ENGLAND

Siddha Yoga Dham London
1 Bonneville Gardens·
London SW4 9LB England
Phone: (01)675-4105

FRANCE

Siddha Yoga Dham France
7 Rue du Plaisir
93400 St. Ouen
Paris, France
Phone: (1)258-51-35

INDIA

Gurudev Siddha Peeth
(WORLD HEADQUARTERS)
P.O. Ganeshpuri (Pin 401 206)
Dist. Thana
Maharashtra, India

**Shree Gurudev Ashram
New Delhi**
Bhatti Village, Mehrauli Block
c/o Khanna, Claridges Hotel
New Delhi South, India 110030

MEXICO

Siddha Yoga Dham Mexico City
Apartado Postal 41-890
Mexico 10 DF Mexico
Phone: (905)286-1676